Mysterious Encounters

UFOs

by Jan Burns

KIDHAVEN PRESS
A part of Gale, Cengage Learning

Detroit • New York • San Francisco • New Haven, Conn • Waterville, Maine • London

LIBRARY OF CONGRESS CATALOGING-IN-PUBLICATION DATA

Burns, Jan.
  UFOs / by Jan Burns.
    p. cm. — (Mysterious encounters)
  Includes bibliographical references and index.
  ISBN 978-0-7377-4048-6 (hardcover)
  1. Unidentified flying objects—Juvenile literature. I. Title.
  TL789.2.B87 2008
  001.942—dc22

                                                              2008006165

KidHaven Press
27500 Drake Rd.
Farmington Hills, MI 48331

ISBN-13: 978-0-7377-4048-6
ISBN-10: 0-7377-4048-5

Printed in the United States of America
2 3 4 5 6 7 12 11 10 09 08

Contents

Chapter 1

Early UFO Sightings

Objects flying through the air that cannot be identified as natural or made by people are called **UFOs**, or unidentified flying objects. Most ancient cultures have stories about mysterious objects seen moving through the sky. Some UFO researchers, or **ufologists,** believe these are the earliest stories of UFOs piloted by **aliens.** Aliens are beings from other planets. Other people claim the sightings were either optical illusions; some sort of natural phenomenon, such as a meteor or a comet; or simply made-up stories. No one knows for sure. This mystery has caused a lot of debate between people who believe in UFOs and those who do not.

Centuries-Old Reports

Writer Raymond Drake believes he has uncovered hundreds of possible reports of ancient UFOs. Citing just a few examples, he says that Romans called them "burning shields." A Sanskrit text described aerial dogfights among gods piloting flying machines called vimanas. During the battles a "blazing missile possessed of the radiance of smokeless fire was discharged." A Chinese tale speaks of a far-off "land of flying carts" inhabited by people riding winged chariots with gilded wheels.[1]

These may only be legends, but Drake points out that legends are often based, at least in part, on fact. Perhaps some of these things were beyond the understanding of the people who lived at that time, and they described the UFOs in terms that were meaningful to their culture.

UFOs in the Bible

Curious passages can also be found in the Bible. The account of Moses leading the Israelites out of Egypt states, "The Lord went before them by day in a pillar of cloud to lead them along the way, and by night in a pillar of fire to give them light, that they might travel by day and by night."[2]

According to Barry H. Downing, the pillars of cloud and fire could have been a UFO, whose exhaust may have parted the Red Sea. Downing's claim at first may seem to be strange, except for the fact that he is a serious biblical scholar as well as a Presbyterian minister. However, as with most ancient writings, there is no way to prove that his claim is true. It is simply his interpretation of the text.

The Bible also tells a story in which the prophet Ezekiel had a vision in 593 B.C. "As I looked, behold, a stormy wind came out of the north and a great cloud, with brightness around it. From the cloud came a structure made up of four sets of sparkling rings and a burning figure."[3] While Ezekiel thought he saw God, some ufologists believe this describes the arrival of an **extraterrestrial** spacecraft.

In the Bible, what Ezekiel thought was God, and some ufologists believe describes the arrival of UFOs, was probably a meteorological event known as a parhelion, or sun dog.

Harvard University astronomer Donald Menzel does not agree. He believes that Ezekiel was tricked by an optical illusion. He thinks that what the prophet Ezekiel described was a rare and complex meteorological event known as a **parhelion**. He suggests that, with a little imagination, its effect is of a huge glistening chariot that is moving with the sun.

Ancient Astronauts

Another intriguing theory comes from writer and former NASA consultant Maurice Chatelain. He says that at Palenque, an ancient Mayan city that lies in Mexico's Yucatán Peninsula, there is a centuries-old pyramid called the Temple of Inscriptions. Inside the temple is a tomb, and on top of the tomb is a surprising stone carving. Chatelain claims that "the very well-preserved [carving] depicts an [ancient] astronaut sitting at the controls of a space vehicle. And it is unmistakably a spacecraft propelled by a jet exhaust."[4] Writer Erich von Daniken agrees with Chatelain's assessment. Describing the carving, he says, "There sits a human being, with the upper part of his body bent forward like a racing motorcyclist; today any child would identify his vehicle as a rocket."[5]

However, archaeologists who have studied the religion of ancient Mexico disagree. They say the carving represents a human's soul moving from life to death. The figure in question is kneeling in front of a sacred tree. The Mayans believed this tree provided a link to the heavens above and the underworld below. They say that Chatelain and von Daniken see what they want to see when looking at the carving. They ignore the meanings Mayans placed on their religious symbols and the style in which they used them.

While these stories and images are intriguing, they happened so long ago that people can only guess at their true meaning. More recent reports contain details that can be analyzed, as in the following cases.

The Battle of Los Angeles

On February 25, 1942, at about 2:30 A.M., the U.S. Army detected an unidentified aircraft. The craft was seen both visually and on radar speeding over the Pacific Ocean heading for Los Angeles. Once the object was over the city, a gigantic sphere was seen glowing

In 1942 witnesses did not believe government reports that a UFO sighting over Los Angeles was only weather balloons.

in the sky. Smaller objects were flying around the large sphere. Antiaircraft guns fired at the objects, but the smaller objects zigzagged back and forth, easily evading the exploding shells. The large sphere was also unharmed. The gun crew fired blast after blast of shells at the unidentified objects for an hour, but none of the objects was hit or shot down. They finally disappeared.

Authorities later claimed the objects were weather balloons. However, witnesses said they did not believe the explanation. Many people observed the objects and did not think they looked anything like weather balloons. Also, if they really were weather balloons, they asked why the balloons were not brought down by the exploding shells.

Finally, in 1987, UFO researcher Timothy Good used the Freedom of Information Act of the United States to obtain a document that Good says had been kept secret for thirty years. It was a memo to

Foo Fighters

Between 1941 and 1945 airmen fighting in Europe during World War II reported seeing strange glowing objects flying around them in the sky. The different shapes included small fireballs of various colors, large red spheres, long cigar-shaped metal objects, and silvery disks. Pilots called these objects *foo fighters*. **It has never been determined exactly what they were.**

President Franklin D. Roosevelt, written the day after the incident by his chief of staff. The document stated that despite the official denials, "unidentified airplanes other than American Army or Navy planes were probably over Los Angeles."[6] While this statement does not say exactly what was over Los Angeles, it does mean they were not weather balloons. No one has ever been able to say for certain what was flying over Los Angeles that day.

A Pilot Sights UFOs

Five years later, on June 24, 1947, businessman Kenneth Arnold was flying his single-engine plane at 9,200 feet (2,804m) over the Cascade Mountains of the state of Washington. As he flew past Mount Rainier he saw a chain of nine peculiar-looking craft flying at high speed across the sky. "I could see their outline quite plainly as they approached the mountain. . . . They were flat like a pie-pan and so shiny that they reflected the sun like a mirror."[7]

Arnold timed them as they flew between two mountains that were about 50 miles (80km) apart. From this he calculated that they were flying at least 1,200 miles per hour (1,931kph), which was faster than any craft at the time could fly. He said, "They flew like a saucer would if you skipped it across the water."[8] Arnold did not mean that the shapes of the objects actually looked like saucers, but reporters at the time described the UFOs that way. This is how the term **flying saucer** started.

At first Arnold guessed that he had witnessed a secret missile test. However, the military later issued a statement saying it had not been testing any new aircraft that day.

A Skeptic's Viewpoint

According to Robert Todd Carroll of the *Skeptic's Dictionary* (http://skepdic.com/ ufos_ets.html), "So far nothing has been positively identified as an alien spacecraft in a way required by common sense and science."

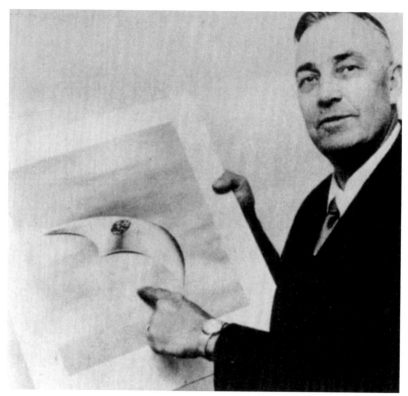

Kenneth Arnold holds a drawing of the UFO he encountered over Mount Rainier, Washington, in 1947.

Arnold's claims were backed up by a prospector who was on nearby Mount Adams at the time. He said the objects were tapered "sharply to a point in the head."[9] As the objects flew overhead they caused his compass needle to move.

Astronomer J. Allen Hynek thinks that Arnold could have misjudged the distance of the objects. He says that they could have been much closer, which would mean they could have been ordinary craft that were flying at a much lower speed than Arnold had thought.

Until the time of Arnold's sighting, UFOs were not taken seriously by most people. No hard evidence had been discovered that proved that UFOs existed. Because of this, despite periodic sightings of UFOs in the sky throughout the world, most claims were dismissed.

That was about to change.

Chapter 2

The Roswell Encounter

A mysterious incident occurred in Roswell, New Mexico, in 1947. It is probably the most famous and the most controversial UFO event in history. More than 50 years have passed, but questions remain about exactly what happened there.

A Strange Discovery

On the night of July 2, 1947, during a violent thunderstorm near Corona, New Mexico, rancher Mac Brazel heard a tremendous explosion. The next day Brazel discovered small pieces of an aluminum-like substance scattered over his pastures. He realized that a craft of some sort must have crashed. Although the lightweight material was thin and flexible, it was extremely tough; he could not bend or cut it. Also, some of the pieces had strange markings on them. He had never seen anything like them before.

He showed some of the debris to Sheriff George Wilcox. Wilcox did not know what to make of them either, so he called the nearby Roswell Army Air Field and notified them about the material.

Investigation

Intelligence officer Major Jessie Marcel was sent out to the crash site to investigate. He later said the wreckage looked like "nothing made on Earth."[10] Because of his training Marcel was familiar with different types of rockets and aircraft, and the debris did not seem like anything that might have come from any of them. He and another officer loaded as much of the material into his Jeep as they could.

Witnesses

Most of the evidence for UFOs comes from eyewitnesses. However, over the years scientists and law enforcement officials have proven that eyewitnesses are usually not reliable at observing, remembering, and reporting what they saw.

Before going back to the base, he went home and showed the remarkable material to his wife and eleven-year-old son. He told them the pieces were from a flying saucer. Marcel's son later said he thought the markings on the material looked like **hieroglyphics**.

Not long afterward Lieutenant Warren Haut, a U.S. Air Force public relations officer at the Roswell base, issued a press release that said, "The many rumors regarding the flying disk became a reality yesterday when the intelligence office of the 509th Bomb Group of the Eighth Air Force,

Children play between two pillars that mark the spot of what many people say was a UFO crash site in Roswell, New Mexico.

UFO Theories

The theory that UFOs come from outer space and are piloted by aliens is known as the extraterrestrial hypothesis. In contrast, the psychosocial hypothesis claims that UFO sightings have a psychological origin. This theory states that people hallucinate (have an imaginary vision that seems real) or misidentify something real, and then they interpret what they have seen according to their social and cultural backgrounds.

Roswell Army Air Field, was fortunate enough to gain possession of a disk through the cooperation of one of the local ranchers and the sheriff's office of Chaves County."[11]

The Story Is Changed

Later that day, however, the base issued a second statement. It said the first story was a mistake, and the object that crashed was actually a high-altitude weather balloon it was testing. These record air temperature and pressure high in the sky. Scientists use them to help predict the weather.

A news conference was held, and Jessie Marcel was shown posed in front of a huge deflated

Many UFO sightings are explained away as strange weather occurrences or weather balloons.

weather balloon. Military personnel at the news conference emphasized again that the report about the flying disk was all a big mistake.

Disbelief and Doubt

Some people did not believe that the wreckage was really from a weather balloon. Members of the Roswell police and fire departments who responded to the crash site also said the weather balloon story was not true. Additionally, some civilians who were initially at the crash site claimed they were threatened by members of the military and were sworn to secrecy about what they saw before they were ordered to leave the site.

Complicating matters, rancher Mac Brazel was kept at the air base for almost a week as he underwent questioning. After he was released he refused to discuss the incident for the rest of his life. Some wondered why all this was necessary if it was only a weather balloon that had crashed.

People started asking all sorts of questions, trying to determine what had really happened. Did Roswell's location have something to do with the incident? Roswell housed the world's only atomic bomber squadron. Two years earlier the first atom bombs had been tested nearby. Also, secret rocket and missile research was carried out at the Roswell Army Air Field. Were experimental craft being tested there? Controversy about the crash died down after a while, but it did not totally go away.

In 1994 the U.S. Air Force, under political pressure, admitted that there had been a cover-up in 1947 in the interest of national security. It said the balloon that had crashed had really been a spy balloon that was part of a military operation known as Project Mogul. Under this program huge high-altitude balloons carried electronic equipment aloft to listen in on Soviet testing of nuclear weapons.

Reporters and others brought up the point that the U.S. Freedom of Information Act has two main provisions. It gives American citizens the right to know about many of their government's activities. However, it also maintains that the president has the right to keep certain matters secret, in the interest of national defense or public policy. Some people questioned if there was more to the Roswell

The secret government military base known as "Area 51" in southern Nevada is thought, by believers, to hold evidence of alien artifacts.

case that was being kept from the public, simply using the excuse of national security.

Witnesses Come Forward

Years after the incident Jessie Marcel claimed that the press conference was faked, and that the weather balloon he posed with was not part of the debris he found on the ranch. He said he had simply followed orders by taking part in the press conference. He also said that in 1947 his superior officers sent troops to guard the crash site and keep curious people away. Then they ordered Marcel to accompany the crash wreckage to Fort Worth, Texas. From there soldiers would transfer it to another plane bound for the Intelligence Center at the Wright-Patterson Air Force Base in Dayton,

Ohio. Afterward, Marcel was ordered to keep quiet about anything related to the crash.

Other people, including military people, who were at the site also came forward years after the incident, finally willing to talk. They claimed that beginning on July 1, 1947, radar had tracked a solid object that seemed to defy conventions because of its speed and maneuverability. At 11:27 P.M. on July 2, radar showed the object pulsating and then exploding into a starburst. The next morning the military moved in and supposedly recovered most of the craft wreckage and bodies of dead aliens, taking them to Wright-Patterson Air Field.

Some ufologists believe the bodies were dissected there and the wreckage examined. However, others think these things were taken to a top-secret military testing ground in Nevada known as Area 51. It was

UFO Expert J. Allen Hynek

Astronomer J. Allen Hynek began as a skeptic, but after studying numerous reports he became convinced that UFOs were real. He was the first person to use the phrase "close encounters of the third kind" to describe encounters between humans and UFOs and/or aliens.

rumored that the military used them there to **reverse engineer** advanced technology. Reverse engineering is the process of working backward from super-advanced technology to arrive at technology that humans can understand and use.

Writer Kevin Randle says that Major Edwin Easley and Sergeant Thomas Gonzales talked to him about the recovery operation. Both men were at Roswell when the crash occurred. They "suggested that the bodies were removed first and that the craft was later taken away."[12] Brigadier General Arthur Exon, who was a lieutenant colonel at the time of the Roswell crash, confirmed that this was true. Although he never saw the bodies or spaceship himself, he talked to people who had done these things and revealed details about them. Exon believes the bodies could still be at Wright-Patterson.

UFO historian David Jacobs and others disagree. They say that if physical evidence of UFOs—such as a craft or its occupants—was found by the government, a large number of scientists and other personnel would probably be needed to examine the material over an extended period. They think it would be extremely difficult to get all these people to keep this secret.

Until top-secret government records about Roswell are declassified and made public, or physical evidence of the UFO is released, it is unlikely that people will know the truth.

Chapter 3

Alien Abductions

Since the early 1960s thousands of people have claimed that they were **abducted** by the alien occupants of UFOs. Skeptics do not believe these reports, saying that the people were either hallucinating or lying. Some UFO researchers, however, believe that aliens could be kidnapping humans and conducting long-term experiments on them, trying to create human-alien hybrids. The case of Betty and Barney Hill is the most famous alien abduction on record.

A Strange Sight

On September 19, 1961, Betty and Barney Hill were driving at night in Indian Head, New Hampshire.

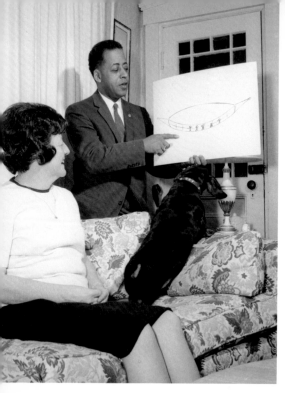

Claiming to have been abducted by aliens, Betty and Barney Hill describe the spaceship that took them prisoner.

They suddenly saw a bright, starlike object moving in the sky. At one point it changed course, curving toward them. It seemed to be following their car. Then, it moved to the right of the highway and hovered there. Barney stopped the car and got out because he wanted to see what kind of plane it was. The UFO responded by moving closer to the car. Barney Hill saw that it was a pancake-shaped craft that had flashing colored lights around the edge. "Hey, I can see a row of windows. There are figures inside," Barney told his wife. "They're looking at us."[13]

The Hills became frightened and quickly drove away. They had not gone far when they heard a beeping nose coming from the trunk of their car. At this point the Hills said they started to feel a tingling sensation throughout their bodies. Later, they realized their journey home took them two hours longer than it should have, but they did not remember anything unusual happening after seeing the UFO. However, Barney's shoes were badly scuffed, and Betty's clothing was stained by a strange pink substance. They had no idea how their things got that way.

Aftermath

That night's events changed their lives forever. Betty started having nightmares about terrifying UFO experiences that she could not explain. In these dreams aliens told her she would have no conscious memory of her abduction. Also, Barney experienced anxiety and insomnia and developed other health problems as well. They decided to seek medical help.

Their doctor recommended they consult psychiatrist Benjamin Simon to see if **hypnotic regression** could help them learn what happened on the night of September 19. They thought it might help

Hypnosis

No one knows for sure if information recovered under hypnosis is true. It could also be confabulation, which is a process in which fantasies based on scraps of actual memory are combined with other material to form a story.

them get their lives back on track. By then, more than two years had passed since the incident.

Simon tape-recorded the interviews so the Hills could hear themselves reveal what had happened. Under deep hypnosis, and interviewed separately, the Hills related that they had been abducted by aliens who were short, gray creatures with large heads and huge, dark eyes. Barney said he remembered being led up a ramp and taken inside a UFO and into an exam room. Then, he said, "I could feel them examining me with their hands."[14]

Betty was able to remember many more details than her husband was, but basically she told a similar story of undergoing a physical examination inside a UFO. "I go into this room . . . and they bring a machine over . . . it's something like a microscope, only a microscope with a big lens. I had an idea they

These signs warn people that they are on the boundary of Area 51.

were taking a picture of my skin."[15] Afterward she asked her captors where they came from and one showed her the location of their home planet on a "star map." Finally, she was released to go back to her car.

Analysis

After their sessions had ended, Simon concluded, "Their story was quite improbable on the basis of any scientific data, but on the other hand it appeared as the case went on that the Hills were not lying, and I felt convinced of that." However, he said, "I was ultimately left with the conclusion that the Hills' experience was the aftermath of some type of experience with an Unidentified Flying Object or some [thing] similar [and that it] assumed the quality of a fantasized experience."[16] Simon said he thought Barney's memory of the UFO experience was a fantasy inspired by Betty's vivid dreams, which she had described to him in detail. However, he admitted this explanation did not totally answer all the questions about their experience.

In the following years many other people experienced similar incidents. These incidents often occurred at night while a person or persons were driving along a deserted road. They spotted the UFO, which often had flashing lights, and soon afterward were transported inside it. Once inside they were given a physical examination and then were released back to their vehicle.

The Hynek UFO Classification System

Type of UFO Sighting

- Nocturnal lights
- Daylight disks
- Radar-visual
- Close encounters of the first kind
- Close encounters of the second kind
- Close encounters of the third kind

Description

- Bright lights seen at night
- Usually oval or disklike
- Those detected by radar
- Visual sightings of an unidentified object
- Visual sightings plus physical effects on animate and inanimate objects
- Sightings of occupants in or around the UFO

More Abductions

In alien abduction cases, the individuals involved often mention lost time, as seen in the case of the Hills. Lost time is often the biggest clue alerting people that something strange has happened to them. This is what happened to the Avis family one night in Aveley, England, in 1974 when they were driving home. They suddenly realized that a pale blue light was following their car. Then, the whole car jolted back and forth. Though they were shaken up, they continued on their way. When they got home, though, they realized that they had arrived three hours later than they should have. To try to learn what had happened during the missing three hours, they agreed to be hypnotized. Their experience turned out to be quite similar to that of the Hills. When questioned under hypnosis, they revealed that they were taken inside a UFO, where aliens performed medical experiments on them.

Charles Hickson (left) and Calvin Paker, involved in the famous Pascagoula abduction case of 1973, claimed they were taken into a spaceship by aliens who had wrinkled skin, a small slit in place of a mouth, no eyes, and claws for hands.

More Lost Time

A slightly different abduction case occurred in December 1967, when police officer Herb Schirmer encountered an egg-shaped object in Ashland, Nebraska. It had tripod legs and was hovering near electrical **pylons**. Afterward, when Schirmer looked at his watch, he realized he could not remember what happened for a twenty-minute span of time. To try to find out what happened, Schirmer allowed himself to be hypnotized by psychologist Leo Sprinkle, who was a leader in the study of UFOs and alien abductions.

Under hypnosis, Schirmer stated that he was forcefully taken aboard a UFO, where aliens were conducting breeding experiments on humans. Before he left, his mind was implanted with a cover story where he would only remember seeing the UFO from afar, instead of actually going on board. Later, Sprinkle said he was convinced that Schirmer "believed in the reality of the events."[17]

Schirmer passed a lie-detector test, but people who did not believe his story pointed out that this did not mean the events actually happened. It simply meant that Schirmer himself believed the events happened.

Hallucinations

Some forms of hallucinations can cause experiences similar to those that people describe in alien abductions. Sleep paralysis, sometimes known as

Folie à Deux

When one person is subconsciously influenced by another, this is known as *folie à deux*. The term is French for "madness of two."

night terrors, can cause feelings of loss of mental and physical control and can be accompanied by a feeling that some threatening menace is nearby. Sleep paralysis is closely related to a particular kind of hallucination known as a **hypnagogic hallucination**. The threat in these situations can take the form of horrifying creatures, among other things.

Most investigators believe that the abductees themselves genuinely believe they were abducted by aliens, although in most cases there is little physical evidence to support their claims. However, more research into alien abduction is necessary to determine what really happens in these situations.

Chapter 4

Looking at Evidence

Studies show that more than 90 percent of all reported UFO sightings have ordinary explanations. They are most likely optical illusions or a **misidentification** of natural or human-made objects. This means that when most people believe they have seen a UFO, they are simply mistaken about what they saw. However, even after investigation, ufologists believe that anywhere from 3 to 8 percent of UFO sightings cannot be explained by any currently known methods. The following cases are examples of these unique types of UFO cases.

The Valentich Incident

Australian pilot Frederich Valentich took off flying a Cessna aircraft over the Bass Strait off the coast of

Victoria, Australia, on October 21, 1978. Before he left, his plane was fueled to capacity, which should have been enough fuel to fly for five hours. The weather was clear, so visibility was excellent.

Forty-seven minutes after taking off, Valentich reported to Melbourne Flight Station controller Steve Robey that a large UFO had suddenly appeared above his plane. He said the craft had a long shape with a green light and that the exterior was shiny and metallic. He asked if there were any other aircraft in the area. Robey told him there were no known aircraft below 5,000 feet (1,524m) in the immediate area. Valentich responded by saying that the object seemed to be "playing some sort of game. He's flying over me two to three times at speeds I cannot identify."[18]

In this famous photo, images of three UFOs fly over the Reichenstein mountain range in Austria, captured by Erich Kaiser while mountain climbing on August 3, 1954.

How Might UFOs Travel?

If UFOs do come from outer space, they would have to travel vast distances in a short period of time. Ideas vary as to how this could be accomplished:

1. UFOs might create an artificial field of gravity in front of them, into which they fall.

2. UFOs could dematerialize and then rematerialize when they reach their destination.

3. UFOs could be nuclear powered and are pushed through space by a stream of radiation.

4. Black holes might offer shortcuts through time and space.

Shortly afterward Robey asked Valentich where the object was at that time. Valentich told him the object was over his airplane. Valentich then announced that he was experiencing engine trouble. After a pause, Valentich then told Robey, "That strange aircraft is on top of me again. . . . It is hovering, and it's not an aircraft."[19] After that Robey heard what sounded like metal scraping against metal. The sound lasted about seventeen seconds, and then there was silence. The entire conversation was recorded by air traffic control.

A search-and-rescue operation was launched when Valentich failed to show up at his destination. Valentich's Cessna was equipped with a radio survival beacon, and it was hoped that the rescuers would be able to pick up the signal. However, no trace of Valentich or any wreckage from his plane was ever found.

There are different ideas about what happened to him. Ufologists believe Valentich and his aircraft were abducted by a giant UFO. Witnesses on the mainland described a number of UFO sightings in the area that day as well as later that night. Also, the coastal area that he took off from had a long history of UFO activity. Controller Steve Robey agrees with this assessment, saying, "Towards the end I think he was definitely concerned for his safety. . . . It was a kind of

These rapidly moving UFOs were filmed in the skies over Mexico by Mexican Air Force pilots on March 5, 2004.

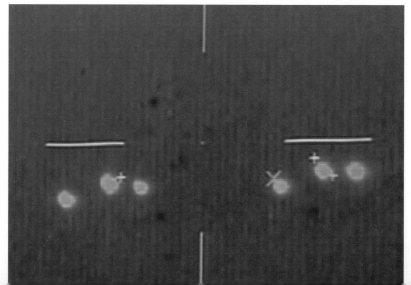

rushed conversation, as if he was startled."[20] Yet aviation authorities disagree. They believe that Valentich may have become disoriented while his plane developed engine problems. They think his craft probably crashed and sank.

The Valentich disappearance remains unsolved.

A Mysterious Sighting

Another unexplained UFO incident occurred on May 11, 1950, when Evelyn Trent was outside in her backyard in McMinnville, Oregon, at about 7:00 P.M. She suddenly saw a huge metallic disk with a flat base gliding silently through the sky. Her husband, Paul Trent, quickly got out a camera and took two photos of the object before it disappeared. The photos turned out to be clear and sharp. Ufologists say the objects in the background of the picture offer perspective, giving viewers a good idea of the distance of the object from the

Many believers offer the McMinnville UFO photographs as proof of the existence of UFOs.

camera. This fact is considered when analyzing photos for any signs of tampering using such things as hidden strings, unusual shadows, or other evidence of falsification.

The Trent pictures so far have proved to be genuine by government scientists who subjected the photos to various tests. They issued this statement about the photos in 1969: "The simplest most direct interpretation of the photographs confirms precisely what the witnesses said they saw." Photo analyst William Hartmann described the object in more detail, saying, "It was an extraordinary flying object, silvery, metallic, disc-shaped, tens of meters in diameter."[21]

Fading In and Out of Reality

Another incident in the same area occurred on November 22, 1966. A college professor with a PhD in biochemistry—who asked to remain anonymous—drove along the Williamette Pass southeast of

Secret Aircraft

People may spot top-secret military planes during test flights and report them as UFOs. The U.S. Stealth bomber was reported as a UFO before its first official flight in 1989.

McMinnville and up into the mountains. He took a series of pictures of the rugged scenery from high up on the mountain at the Diamond Peak viewing area.

After taking the photos he saw something fuzzy out of the corner of his eye. He took another photo before the object vanished skyward. He was not sure if he had really seen anything or not. When the film was developed, something unexpected turned up on one of the photos. It showed what appeared to be a disk-shaped object with a flat base that was about 22 feet (6.7m) in diameter.

Three images of the UFO appear in a single frame as the UFO rises from the snow-clad trees. Researchers who have examined it suggest the object may have faded in and out of reality while the camera's shutter was open. UFO expert Adrian Vance believes the picture proves that UFOs behave in a manner completely outside that of normal physical aircraft. He says its motion is not unlike what happens at the quantum level of subatomic physics, where ghost particles fade in and out of reality in rapid succession.

These photos are some of the few UFO photos that show no signs of tampering, even today. This is important because today's sophisticated testing

Some people feel that crop circles are made by UFOs during their landings on Earth, but there is greater evidence that most are man-made.

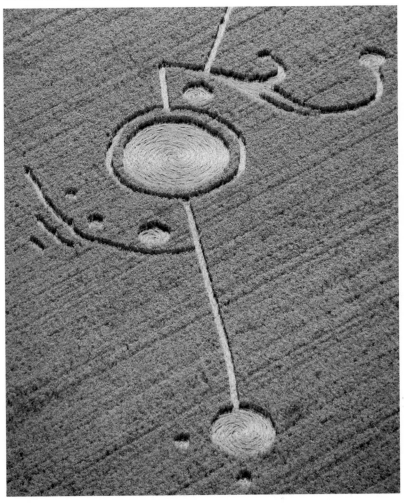

equipment has revealed that many of the early UFO pictures were faked, although they were believed to be real at the time they were first examined.

Continuing Investigation

Rigorous testing, in fact, is the norm for UFO investigations today. The situation has changed dramatically from tests done in the 1940s in which untrained

UFO expert Dr. J. Allen Hynek.

Public Opinion

In 2002 a Roper poll commissioned by the Sci Fi Channel found that nearly half of those surveyed believe that UFOs have visited Earth in some form over the years. About 70 percent of those surveyed believe the government has not told the public everything it knows about UFOs.

investigators used simple methods. There are now standard methods for collecting and analyzing data, photos, and other evidence. UFO reports are not automatically accepted as true. They are thoroughly reviewed.

Many of these improvements are due to the influence of astronomer and UFO investigator J. Allen Hynek. He suggested that cases be given serious study by trained scientists. He also thought that the information in the case reports should be shared among investigating groups so that the information, such as UFO colors, shapes, geographical concentrations, and speeds, could be analyzed. Hynek predicted that the explanation for UFOs, when it is finally discovered, "will prove to be not merely the next small step in the march of science but a mighty and totally expected quantum jump."[22]

Notes

Chapter 1: Early UFO Sightings

1. Quoted in Pat Daniels, ed., *The UFO Phenomenon*. Alexandria, VA: Time-Life, 1987, p. 12.

2. Quoted in Daniels, *The UFO Phenomenon*, p. 12.

3. Quoted in Daniels, *The UFO Phenomenon*, p. 12.

4. Quoted in Michael Arvey, *UFOs*. San Diego: Greenhaven, 1989, p. 39.

5. Quoted in Arvey, *UFOs*, p. 39.

6. Quoted in Jenny Randles, *UFOs and How to See Them*. New York: Sterling, 1992, p. 11.

7. Quoted in Arvey, *UFOs*, p. 48.

8. Quoted in Arvey, *UFOs*, p. 48.

9. Quoted in *UFO Hunters*, "Kenneth Arnold," History.com. www.history.com/minisite.do?content_type=Minisite_Generic&content_type_id=54948&display_order=2&mini_id=54840.

Chapter 2: The Roswell Encounter

10. Quoted in Eric Elfman, *Almanac of Alien Encounters*. New York: Random House, 2001, p. 28.

11. Quoted in Daniels, *The UFO Phenomenon*, p. 39.

12. Quoted in Kevin Randle, *The Randle Report: UFOs in the '90s*. New York: M. Evans, 1997, p. 155.

Chapter 3: Alien Abductions

13. Quoted in Philip Brooks, *Invaders from Outer Space: Real-Life Stories of UFOs.* London: DK, 1999, p. 20.

14. Quoted in Daniels, *The UFO Phenomenon,* p. 82.

15. Quoted in Daniels, *The UFO Phenomenon,* p. 84.

16. Quoted in Arvey, *UFOs,* p. 85.

17. Quoted in Randles, *UFOs and How to See Them,* p. 29.

Chapter 4: Looking at Evidence

18. Quoted in UFO Area, "The Disappearance of Frederich Valentich," 2000. www.ufoarea. com/events_valentich.html.

19. Quoted in UFO Area, "The Disappearance of Frederich Valentich."

20. Quoted in Daniels, *The UFO Phenomenon,* p. 138.

21. Quoted in Randles, *UFOs and How to See Them,* p. 60.

22. Quoted in Daniels, *The UFO Phenomenon,* p. 144.

Glossary

abducted: Kidnapped and held against one's will.

aliens: Creatures from another planet.

confabulation: A process in which fantasies based on scraps of actual memory are combined with other material to form a story.

extraterrestrial: A being or thing from beyond Earth.

flying saucer: A mysterious object that may come from outer space. Such objects are now known as UFOs.

hieroglyphics: A picture or symbol that stands for a word, syllable, or sound. The ancient Egyptians and others used such pictures instead of an alphabet.

hypnagogic hallucination: A particular kind of hallucination that is closely related to sleep paralysis.

hypnotic regression: A type of hypnosis in which participants are led to reveal past events.

misidentification: Identifying something incorrectly.

parhelion: A rare and complex meteorological event that causes unusual light effects in the sky.

pylons: High towers, used for holding up electric lines.

reverse engineer: To work backward from superadvanced alien technology to arrive at technology that humans can understand and use.

ufologist: A UFO researcher.

UFOs: Unidentified flying objects.

For Further Exploration

Books

Eric Elfman, *Almanac of Alien Encounters*. New York: Random House, 2001. This is an interesting book with many stories and examples of possible alien encounters, from prehistory to the present.

Judith Herbst, *UFOs*. Minneapolis: Lerner, 2005. This book provides general information about UFOs, along with possible explanations for them.

Janet Stirling, *UFOs*. New York: Rosen, 2002. This book examines case studies and reports of UFO encounters.

Web Sites

The Skeptic's Dictionary (http://skepdic.com/ufos_ets.html). On this Web site, skeptic Robert Todd Carroll offers a nonbeliever's perspective of UFO evidence.

UFO Evidence (www.ufoevidence.org). This is one of the Internet's largest sources of research and information on the UFO phenomenon, with more than two thousand articles, documents, and resources.

Index